Three Weeks in the City

Adam Lemieux

BookLeaf
Publishing

Presentation by *BookLeaf Publishing*

Web: www.bookleafpub.com

E-mail: info@bookleafpub.com

ISBN: 978-93-95890-05-2

First edition 2022

*To every living thing that has crossed my
path.*

PREFACE

However long or short these poems are, I did try
to say something with each one--whether or not
I did is up to you.

The Littered Streets

Walking down an unlit alley
I find a single shoe and a rusty muffler.
Displaced members of society,
what are they doing here?

How have these objects, inanimate but alive,
found the ground I currently tread?

I think of all the socks lost in dryers
riding the tunnels and sewers of cities
and washing up on curbs
crumpled and still dirty.

The floods of miscellanea
littering the streets
despite the bylaw signs.

Rules are meant to be broken, they say,
but no one is playing the same game,
especially those picked last at everything.
Discarded afterthoughts.

Now they lie on the roads and the paths
of those with sneering faces,

and with email complaints on their fingertips,
asking what they pay taxes for anyways.

The shoe and muffler remain,
not where they're supposed to be.
I leave them alone because
where is anyone supposed to be?

Waiting For The Storm on Story Three

Outside the window,
a fierce, cool breeze
ruffles the canopy
of the swaying elm tree.

The darkened clouds unite
to cover the sliver of sky
that overhangs this life
inside.

A rumble in the distance,
quakes louder than the window shaker,
forewarning the instance
when the rain hits.

When it will wash away the dirt
from my windows, my fire escape,
reinvigorate the Earth,
and make nature squeal with mirth.

And then a flash of light.
(or trick of the eye).
Before I see or feel the plight,
I hear the shower, recite.

What if a mountain was only a hill?

The colossal obstacles constantly
blocking your progress,
reduced to mere mounds of minutiae.
The life-altering issues
derailing your days,
no longer holding any sway.

What if those mountains were always hills,
bloated by imagination,
or social expectation?

We make them insurmountable,
and so they are.

In the city of Hamilton,
they call a hill a mountain.
Once, representing opportunity,
growth,
a sense of making it.
Now it sits, conquered,
background noise,
as common as the people it holds.

All climbs are dreadful,
until your hand touches down
on top,
and pushes the weight
that once rode on your shoulders
to underneath your feet.

The Unplanned City

Miniature skylines of ripped out pages:
Peaks and valleys, and paper skyscrapers
Formed by forgotten ideas for the world.

They are what was, and what could have been,
Lodged forever between potential.

A reminder of crumpled subjectivity.

The Meter's Running

The meter's running, says the cab driver.
You don't hear that anymore these days.
He looks at me in the rearview mirror.
Cause we pay for Uber on our phones.
I see his mouth curl, slightly amused.

My meter's running away from me,
I tell him as I hold back a sigh.
His neck pivots towards me this time,
And I smile back expectantly.
He says: what on earth do you mean?

I say: I'm trying to write a poem.
He asks why on earth would I do that.
(At times like these I have no clue–)
You're right I should probably quit.
It seems to be the end of his offering.

And then he says: I don't get poetry–
It always reads like nothing to me.
(Nothing? It can never mean just nothing.)
I close my journal and look away.
Sometimes that's all it is.

Best Friends Forever

She was the fun girl on the street,
we let the sparks unfurl between us–
the flint to an unseen fire.

Playing cards in tire spokes,
chasing after ice cream trucks,
and finding sticks disguised as magic wands.

Knocking on front doors,
asking for sidekicks and co-captains
for treasure hunts and space missions.

Pleading with parents
just to play,
imaginations untethered by what should be.

Days pass easy with no cares;
only unearthing nooks and crannies,
and forgotten places.

Giving names to the faces
built into buildings, and tree trunks
and car headlights.

When we kissed,
it was for experiment–
we laughed cause it was gross.

Childhood best friends
forever,
if only just in memory.

The library
of our created stories
echo for eternity.

Hanging in the Backyard

Lights strewn from the telephone pole,
to the rundown shed,
to the awning overhead.

Fitted sheets and beach towels
rock gently,
pinned to the aging clothesline.

Potted plants on ornate hooks,
reach for the arcing sun,
and quiver from an earlier spray.

Wooden windchimes
sing their hollow song,
seemingly keeping the rats away.

A family moves tiny helpings to their plates
and share their days,
slowly melting into cushioned seats.

Until a Man Accepts

Until a man accepts his glory days
have a different definition now,
he'll revel in the athletic prowess of his youth,
gather on Saturday mornings
to play touch football,
to be uncouth, away from his wife and kids
and feel the way he did on Friday nights
when he was in school,
when he was cool,
when the girls and boys would drool,
as he walked around protected
by the shield of possibility–
where only good things were going to happen,
because they normally did,
to him.
Until a man accepts his glory days
have a different definition now,
he'll continue reaching backwards
through the haze of reminiscence to validate
a well-lived life.

The In/Consequential Things
We Do When We're Nine

When I was nine, I transferred schools.
Week One:
These boys, whose names I don't recall,
sought out the weak one,
and I wanted to fit in
because I was new, and because I was nine.

It was snowing,
so like us, the other boy wore a hat–
And just like that–
It was plucked from his head,
As he went shoulder first into a hardened pile.

A game of keep-away ensued,
monkey in the middle, he chased his hat around.
For how long, I do not know,
but not long, for fear of being caught.
We left the boy, distraught.

Of course he told on us,
'Tattled' in those days.
He was nine as well,
So what did we expect?

An after school detention was called
To discuss our bully quest;
Many excuses were thrown around,
But mine, for sure, was lousiest:
"The wind took it, as I tried to give it back."

As if I meant to give back those four days
of popularity I had tested out.
I didn't know,
and don't remember now
what I was thinking.
Or even what the punishment was.

.

.

.

The irony of the situation:

The boy,

The un-hatted one,

Became my best friend,

For many years.

Behind the Neon Sign

In the hotel room behind the neon sign,
through the translucent sheers,
it is perpetual daytime.

An uninvited rival to the purpose of the room–
how am I to sleep,
when my eyeballs think it's noon?

My dreams mimic the tossing and turning of my
body.
I want to learn their meaning,
but the outer light keeps me foggy.

I wake up every hour, maybe every two,
and glare at that blasted window,
as it glares back at me, unmoved.

I spring out of bed, since I'm fully awake
to consider my plans for the pane;
and that's when I notice the fabric, opaque.

Oh…

The New Animal Kingdom

15

In the paved jungle
of the new animal kingdom,
they move at a snail's pace
in the race to get home.
Honking away,
the geese (the new lions)
have come to feast
on the tiny metal shells
that leave a trail of slime
behind.
Four circles of life beneath
the beasts
carry them farther into strife–
the spoils go to those
who only fend for themselves.

The Siren Song for Flies

In the woods held up by nails and screws,
the fly buzzes around, tipsy on the good life.

Safe from the dangers of the outside world,
he grows accustomed to the continued quiet.

He heads for an apple in this garden of eden
and lands beside it, wafting in the sweet aroma.

Enchanted, entranced, enthralled, enraptured,
he doesn't hear the whoosh or the ensuing splat.

Thus is the end for the fly,
fat and happy on the counter he lies.

The Cottage Sweater

The cottage sweater should be oversized,
enough room inside
to never feel confined.

It should smell like bug spray and campfires,
like the musk of cedar and pine,
of freshly brewed coffee,
and homemade red wine.

It should always be there, like the space
between mom and dad
after a nightmare.

It could be hand-made,
It could give you an itch,
It could be horribly frayed,
It could be missing a stitch.

It should be well-worn,
like the cottage,
and the rest of its contents.

It should be full of fresh air,
and starry nights
without clouds.

It should feel like home
away from home
away from home.

Labour Day Weekend

The white caps rumble on a Lake Erie beach,
people gather for the last long weekend of
summer.

Cold weather is on the horizon,
but today it's bright and blinding.
Peculiarly titled Labour Day,
as thoughts of work are kept at bay,
(Autumn is three weeks away).

No more water, the warmest it'll be,
no more sky, the bluest they will see.
the last time sand will be stuck between toes,
the last time skin will be sun kissed,
(Until next year that is).

The last day a swimsuit will be daily wear,
the last day it's easy to be friends with strangers.
the last weekend of summer, how they dread its
arrival.
but without the dread,
they wouldn't make the most of their time here.

Writer's Blocks

What am I in this little box,
on the corner of Hunter and Emerald?
I am green with envy–
I watch the city blow up around me.
I am disconnected from the streets,
the talking pavement,
the bellowed words from below
are all that reach the open window of my seat;
they do nothing for the heat.
I can't wear shirts, or pants,
cause they only cause sweat,
And I have enough to fret about.
The casing of my pen melts away,
leaving smudges on my fingers–
the idea that I'm nothing lingers.

The Plot is There

21

Behind a metal shed, at the end
of a four car driveway,
lies a plot
with rhubarb and Lily of the Valley.
Next to it lies a black compost bin
churning out nourished soil
for the lot.
Most often the rhubarb is left to die,
life filling up too quickly
before it can be baked into pies.
The Lily of the Valley spreads
like the arms of the grandmother
who loves it dearly
to every inch of the dirt,
leaving no room for the flirting weeds.
This tender patch of green
cannot be seen from the road,
but it's there,
and somebody should know.

Who Am I Today?

Who will I meet today,
and who will I subsequently be?
What language will my body speak?
How will my voice perform?

Can I muster the air of confidence,
as if I was talking to myself,
or will I stumble and fall,
and say things I do not mean?

How many versions of a person can there be?
Perhaps the same amount as people that I see.
Endless presentations of one self,
yet none the truest.

The fear of showing the at-home-alone,
comfortable-in-his-own-skin,
free-as-a-bird depiction,
too much to overcome.

Smarthomes, Smartphones...

Smartclones copying the trends
pretending it's theirs–
where does it start, where does it end?

Camera doorbells
tell us who's there
without moving from our chairs.

We know our first dates from before
when we scoped out their lives
on social platforms.

All the answers in our pockets,
so what's the point of questions?
We are content to look at content.

This poem is a clone.
You've read all this before,
and you will read it again.

The Intersection of Summer and Fall

It's the season of peeling back layers,
of cold mornings and hot afternoons,
of looking ahead and being prepared
as the end of the year approaches.

It's the season of adapting to the times,
of fresh starts and accepting unknowns,
of digging deep and finding the whys,
in spite of the ever fading light.

It's the season to become,
to be humble and to be one with nature,
to love the themes that are apparent,
and see inner circles more often.

It's the season of anticipation,
of easing into imminent challenges,
of perfect timing
and making the most of it.

It's the season to fall.
It's the season to get up.

This Poem's Life

How do I animate a poem?

How do I give it a brain to imagine
beautiful imagery and express that scenery
in perfectly crafted words?

How do I give it the eyes to see
all the specificities it would miss if
it stayed blindfolded on the desk?

How do I give it the mouth to speak
to reach the ears of the people
who want to consume and digest it?

How do I give it the heartbeat, the rhythm,
the cadence that signifies the life blood
that flows inside its form?

How do I give it the stomach to accept
the harsh realities of not being liked
by all who read?

How do I give it the balls to say something
controversial and be open for discussion
about why it's right or wrong?

How do I give it the legs to stand up
and support itself after I've moved on
and forgotten it?

How do I give it the feet to walk a thousand
miles
and understand the stamina required
to be remembered?

How do I animate a poem?

Looking Back

27

After all this time,
I still look in the mirror
and reflect.